Collins

easy learning

English

quick quizzes

Ages 5–7

Helen Cooper

Context cues

Choose the correct word to finish each sentence.

sister	walk	picnic	drums
play	flies	cricket	dishes
money	going		

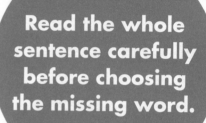
Read the whole sentence carefully before choosing the missing word.

1 Which girl is your _____?

2 I take my dog for a _____ every day.

3 I love having a _____ on a sunny day.

4 Spiders catch _____ in webs.

5 My brother's favourite sport is _____.

6 I have no _____ left in my purse.

7 Tomorrow we are _____ on holiday.

8 After tea, I have to wash the _____.

9 She can _____ the guitar.

10 He can play the _____.

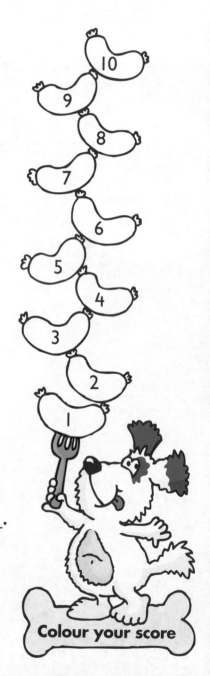

Colour your score

2

Word building

Rearrange the groups of letters to build words.

Say the sounds aloud. Then say them in different orders.

1 p   ee   sh   _____

2 s   t   oa   c   _____

3 igh   t   m   _____

4 sh   t   ir   _____

5 t   or   sp   _____

6 ng   i   th   _____

7 ch   t   a   _____

8 ch   u   n   l   _____

9 d   n   i   w   _____

10 l   ai   s   n   _____

11 er   ow   t   _____

12 l   oi   f   _____

13 oo   s   t   b   _____

14 ll   e   sh   _____

15 r   i   b   ck   _____

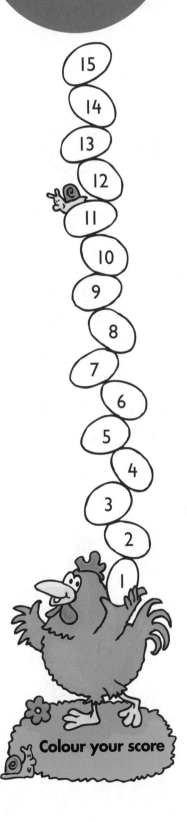

15
14
13
12
11
10
9
8
7
6
5
4
3
2
1

Colour your score

3

Vowel digraphs

Choose a vowel digraph to complete the word.

ai ee oa oo oi ie ou

1

t___l

2

cl___d

3

bl___d

4

ch___se

5

cl___k

6

sn___l

7

t___

8

n___l

9

c___n

10

m___se

11

gr___n

12

l___p

A digraph has two letters, but makes one sound.

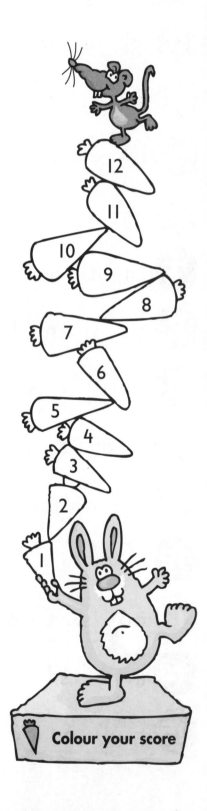

12
11
10
9
8
7
6
5
4
3
2
1

Colour your score

Real or made-up?

Sort the words into the boxes.

1 shop
2 shup
3 church
4 grirk
5 zirn
6 girl
7 frud
8 frog

9 hild
10 hill
11 door
12 druft
13 week
14 walk
15 thurp

Being able to sound a word out doesn't make it real.

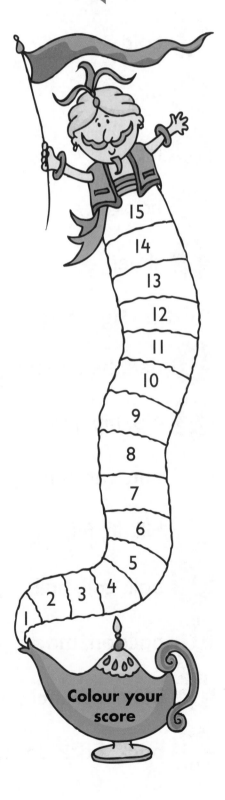

Real words	Made-up words

15
14
13
12
11
10
9
8
7
6
5
4
3
2
1

Colour your score

Rhyming words

Draw a line between each pair of rhyming words.

The final sound of the word makes the rhyme.

1 band   keep

2 ring   book

3 cold   jig

4 wig   pet

5 let   hold

6 hook   king

7 sheep   hand

Add a rhyming word to each list.

8 den, hen, pen, _____

9 dip, hip, pip, _____

10 but, cut, hut, _____

11 bill, ill, fill, _____

12 ball, call, hall, _____

13 balloon, moon, _____

14 bunch, crunch, hunch, _____

15 back, hack, Jack, _____

14
13
15
12
11
10
9
8
7
6
5
4
3
2
1

Colour
your score

Common exception words

Find the words in the list hidden in the grid.

They can go across or down the grid.

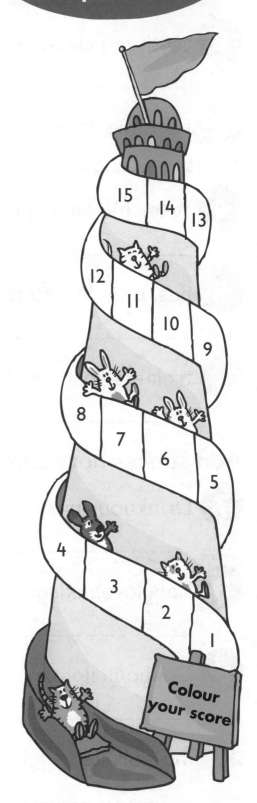

Learn to read and spell these words. They will come up a lot.

1. said
2. today
3. because
4. are
5. our
6. they
7. you
8. were
9. friend
10. where
11. come
12. was
13. some
14. there
15. she

s	a	i	d	a	t	o	d	a	y
y	t	z	s	o	m	e	c	t	w
w	r	f	r	i	e	n	d	h	e
b	e	c	a	u	s	e	o	e	r
s	m	o	h	u	o	m	t	r	e
h	c	m	n	o	u	r	h	e	a
e	l	e	w	h	e	r	e	h	q
a	r	e	w	a	s	h	y	o	u

Colour your score

Sentences

Rewrite these sentences so that they make sense.

1 I like don't my hair. washing

_____

2 teeth my clean I every day.

_____

3 I orange drink juice. breakfast, At

_____

4 sister My bike. a ride can

_____

5 bus. a on We to town went

_____

6 trainers. lost his He has

_____

Add spaces between the words.

7 Drinkyourmilk.

_____

8 Theylovebakingcakes.

_____

9 Canyouhelpme?

_____

10 Ihavebrokenmyglasses.

_____

The capital letters and full stops will give you a clue.

Colour your score

10 9 8 7 6 5 4 3 2 1

8

Alphabetical order

Put these letters in alphabetical order.

1 d c b a _____

2 f i e g _____

3 h l m k _____

4 q p o n _____

5 u t r s w _____

6 x v z y _____

Which word comes first alphabetically?

7 ball or fish? _____

8 television or radio? _____

9 apple or orange? _____

10 hat or gloves? _____

11 knife or fork? _____

12 saucer or cup? _____

13 scooter or bike? _____

14 pencil or ruler? _____

15 cushion or pillow? _____

Learn the order of the letters in the alphabet.

Colour your score

15
14
13
12
11
10
9
8
7
6
5
4
3
2
1

Word meanings

Draw a line to match each meaning to the correct noun.

1 Something you wear on your head.

2 An orange vegetable.

3 Food from Italy.

4 Something you wear on your feet.

5 Something you write with.

6 A piece of furniture that you sit on.

pen

pasta

chair

carrot

hat

shoes

Use a dictionary if you are not sure what a word means.

Choose a word to match each meaning.

ball   fridge   fish   bed

7 A round object that you can bounce. _____

8 You keep things cool in this. _____

9 You sleep in this. _____

10 These animals live in water. _____

Colour your score

Features of stories

Write **character, setting** or **plot** alongside each example.

The plot is the story. The setting is where it takes place.

1 Goldilocks _____

2 A cottage _____

3 A boy wants to
make some money _____

4 A castle _____

5 A wolf wants to
eat Grandma _____

6 A wicked wizard _____

Does each phrase usually come at
the **beginning** or the **end** of a story?
Circle your answer.

7 Once upon
a time **beginning / end**

8 They all lived
happily ever after **beginning / end**

9 Long, long ago **beginning / end**

10 And he was never
seen again **beginning / end**

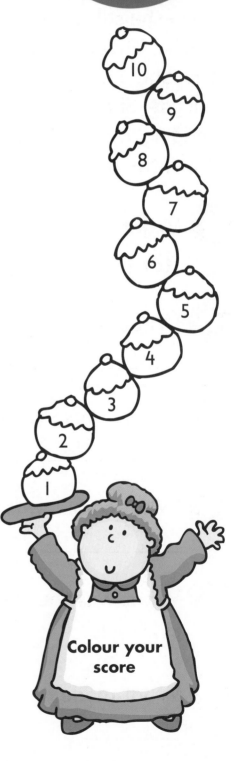

Colour your
score

11

Comprehension

Read this passage carefully and then answer the questions.

I know a little girl called Goldilocks. She likes peeping in other people's houses. One day she was playing in the woods. She saw a cottage with a bright yellow door. She went inside and saw three bowls of porridge on the table. She quickly ate a bowl. Then she sat down on a soft, red chair. She went upstairs to have a look. There were three beds. She lay down on a small green bed. She quickly fell asleep. She woke up when she heard voices outside. She looked out of the window. The three bears were heading for the front door. She opened the window and climbed down the drain pipe. Then she ran away as fast as she could!

1 What is the name of the girl in the story? _____

2 What does she like to do?

_____

3 Where was she playing?

_____

4 What colour was the cottage's door?

_____

5 What was the chair that she sat on like? _____

6 What made her wake up?

_____

Types of sentence

What type of sentence is it?
Write statement, command,
question or exclamation.

Different types of
sentence need different
punctuation.

1 Have you ever been
to France? _____

2 What a horrible thing
to happen! _____

3 Go to bed. _____

4 I have some new pyjamas. _____

5 Why are you looking
at me like that? _____

6 How lovely to see you! _____

7 Brush your teeth. _____

Finish each sentence with the correct
punctuation mark.

8 Do you want to help me cook lunch

9 What a mess you've made

10 Put the book on the shelf

11 I like cooking

12 How many eggs do I need

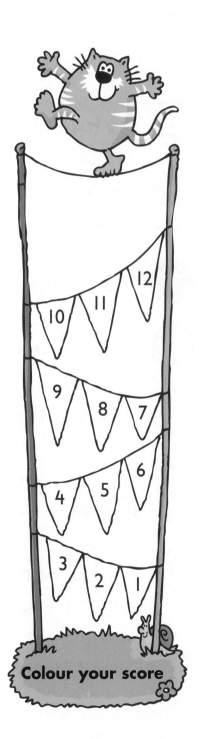

Colour your score

Present tense

Circle the correct verb.

1. I like to **watch** / **watches** television.

2. Hal **reads** / **read** in bed every night.

3. I **uses** / **use** a torch to read.

4. Eva **love** / **loves** going to her grandparents' house.

5. We love to play outside when it **rain** / **rains**.

6. My aunt **send** / **sends** me a present for my birthday every year.

7. They **wants** / **want** to go into town.

8. My friend **draw** / **draws** brilliantly.

9. My uncle likes to go **fish** / **fishing**

10. My mum and I like to practise **singing** / **sing**.

11. We are **eating** / **eat** curry for dinner tonight.

12. Grandma is **cut** / **cutting** the lawn.

Use the present tense to talk or write about something that is happening now.

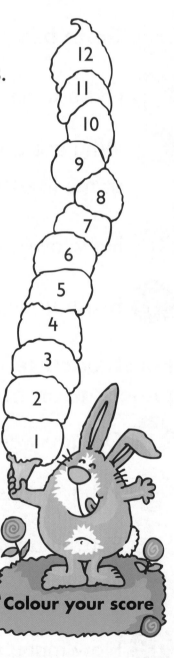

Colour your score

12
11
10
9
8
7
6
5
4
3
2
1

Past tense

Circle the past tense of each verb.

The past tense means something has already happened.

1. go   **went**
2. **was**   am
3. skip   **skipped**
4. grow   **grew**
5. **dug**   dig
6. write   **wrote**

Underline the sentence that has the correct past tense.

7. Yesterday, I goed to school.
   Yesterday, I went to school.

8. I eated spaghetti for lunch.
   I ate spaghetti for lunch.

9. Last week, I saw a film at the cinema.
   Last week, I seed a film at the cinema.

10. Last year, I flew to Canada.
    Last year, I flied to Canada.

11. My sister travel to Liverpool.
    My sister travelled to Liverpool.

12. I sang in a choir last month.
    I sunged in a choir last month.

Colour your score

15

Correct sentences

Tick (✓) the sentence if the capital letters and full stops are correct. Put a cross (✗) if not.

Sentences start with a capital letter and often end with a full stop.

1 Ed and Alfie are making a film. ☐

2 mya and emmie enjoy playing computer games. ☐

3 Poppy and Kitty have a new bedroom. ☐

4 Bella and Eli are twins ☐

5 ava and sara are fantastic runners. ☐

6 Max and Millie make a lot of noise. ☐

7 abu and Ayesha walk to school every day. ☐

8 Cameron and heather cycle home ☐

9 he is a doctor. ☐

10 We went to Portugal on holiday. ☐

10
9
8
7
6
5
4
3
2
1

Colour your score

Questions

Write the correct word to complete each question.

In wh words, the h is silent, but don't forget to write it.

1 _____ is she talking to?
Who   What   Where   When

2 _____ is he holding?
Why   What   How   Will

3 _____ are you going?
Who   Does   Where   Do

4 _____ you count to 100?
Who   Why   Can   When

5 _____ one is your favourite?
Which   Is   Do   What

6 _____ many people are in your class? **How   When   Will   Is**

7 _____ coat is this?
Who   Where   Whose   Can

8 _____ your cat chase mice?
Do   Where   Does   Why

9 _____ you lend me your pen?
Who   What   Will   Do

10 _____ Canada bigger than Australia?
Will   Do   Is   Can

10
9
8
7
6
5
4
3
2
1

Colour your score

Exclamation marks

Tick (✓) the sentence if it needs an exclamation mark. Put a cross (✗) if not.

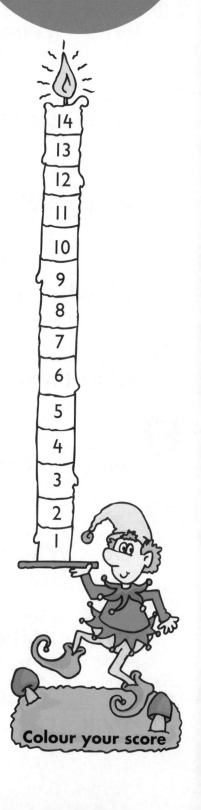

Use an exclamation mark when something is funny, scary, loud or exciting.

1 How many boys are coming to your party! ☐

2 I go to school! ☐

3 Wow! That is amazing! ☐

4 That's the best present ever! ☐

5 He likes running! ☐

6 It's a goal! ☐

7 Two plus two equals four! ☐

8 I can't wait! ☐

Finish these sentences with an exclamation mark or a full stop.

9 I eat cheese sandwiches

10 I'm so angry with them

11 My dad is the best dad in the world

12 We will be there at 2 o'clock

13 That's the best joke I have ever heard

14 Don't do that

Colour your score

Proper nouns

Sort these nouns into the correct boxes. Give them a capital letter if needed.

1 apple

2 wales

3 fork

4 car

5 emily

6 amsterdam

7 sock

8 wednesday

9 september

10 grass

11 dan

12 arthur

13 feather

14 string

15 india

> The names of people, places, days and months need capital letters.

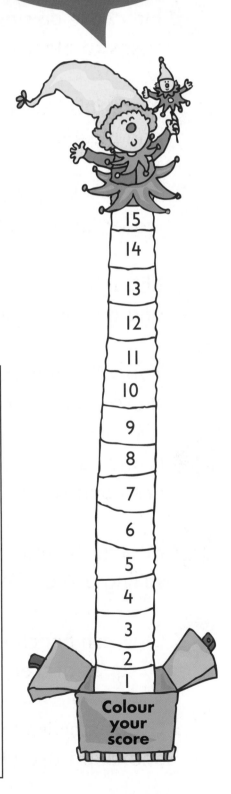

Capital letters needed	Capital letters not needed

15
14
13
12
11
10
9
8
7
6
5
4
3
2
1
Colour your score

Commas in lists

Add commas to the lists in these sentences.

1. We had to travel by car boat plane and train to get there.

2. He chose daisies poppies lilies and roses to plant in the garden.

3. Materials like metal paper glass and plastic can be recycled.

4. The drinks menu included coffee water juice and tea.

5. I bought new gloves a scarf a hat and a coat in the sale.

6. You will need paint paintbrushes a sketch book and glue.

7. France Spain Germany and Italy are countries in Europe.

8. Running swimming cycling and sailing are all Olympic sports.

9. Oak ash beech elder and elm are all types of tree.

10. Crabs starfish lobsters shrimps and clams are all sea creatures.

Do not put a comma before the word and in a list.

Colour your score

20

Contractions

Rewrite these as contractions.

1 She will _____

2 He is _____

3 I am _____

4 We can not _____

5 They should not _____

6 You have _____

7 It is _____

Write out the contractions in full.

8 <u>She's</u> a star. _____

9 He <u>didn't</u> eat lunch. _____

10 <u>We're</u> wet. _____

11 <u>He'll</u> help you. _____

12 <u>You're</u> very untidy. _____

13 <u>They're</u> not going. _____

14 <u>We've</u> no money. _____

15 <u>I'll</u> do the shopping. _____

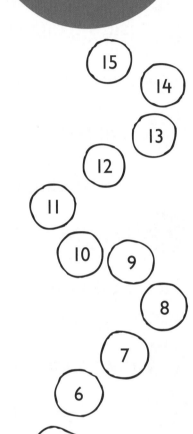

The apostrophe takes the place of one or more letters.

Colour your score

Possessive apostrophes

Circle the possessive apostrophes.

1. Caleb's coat is wet.

2. Darcey's hair is long.

3. Isla's trainers are dirty.

4. Evie's flute was a birthday present.

5. Gabriel's jumper is red.

6. We're playing with Hamza's ball.

7. They're having a lift in Jordan's car.

Put a possessive apostrophe in each of these sentences.

8. Mums cake is delicious.

9. The dogs tail is very long.

10. Eleanors scarf is black and white.

11. Fayes scooter is silver.

12. Arthurs bag is huge!

13. The elephants trunk squirted out water.

14. The cars horn kept tooting.

15. Toms skates flashed in the sun.

A possessive apostrophe shows that something belongs to someone.

15 14 13 12 11 10 9 8 7 6 5 4 3 2 1

Colour your score

22

Plural nouns

Write the plural of each word.

1 Some _____

2 Some _____

3 Some _____

4 Some _____

5 Some _____

6 Some _____

7 Some _____

8 Some _____

Add s or es to make these words plural.

9 wish___

10 lunch___

11 box___

12 rock___

13 dress___

14 monkey___

15 bunch___

Add **es** to words ending **s**, **ss**, **x**, **z**, **zz**, **ch** or **sh** to make them plural.

Colour your score

Conjunctions

Choose a conjunction to complete each sentence.

Conjunctions join parts of a sentence.

when	because	and	if	but
	that	or		

1 The washing machine has finished _____ it keeps beeping.

2 She chose that one _____ it is red.

3 They were just about to leave _____ they heard a scream.

4 _____ there is any left, I will eat it.

5 Bea likes ice-cream _____ Lottie doesn't.

6 This is the dog _____ bit my brother.

7 Would you like to play skipping _____ football?

8 We missed the start of the film _____ we were late.

9 Would you like pasta _____ rice?

10 We will go out _____ your sister has put her shoes on.

Colour your score

10 9 8 7 6 5 4 3 2 1

24

Homophones

Draw a line to match each pair of homophones.

Learn the differences in spelling and meaning between the homophones.

1 sun   too

2 bear   beech

3 see   their

4 blue   hare

5 hair   son

6 beach   sea

7 two   bare

8 there   blew

Circle the correct homophone.

9 Can you **here / hear** me?

10 Do you **know / no** my friend?

11 At **night / knight**, I can see the moon.

12 I need a new **pear / pair** of shoes.

13 **For / Four** is the number after three.

14 They went for a swim in the **see / sea**.

Colour your score

25

Adjectives

Circle the adjective in each sentence.

1 The tiny seed fell onto the soil.

2 The red hen planted it.

3 The yellow corn grew.

4 The nasty wolf wanted to eat grandma.

5 The grumpy troll lived under the bridge.

6 The goat looked at the juicy grass.

7 Goldilocks loved sweet porridge.

8 The fox helped the gingerbread man.

Circle the best adjective.

9 The carrot was **sharp / furry / orange**.

10 The **purple / hard / sticky** glue went all over my shirt.

11 The **bendy / angry / cold** man shook his fist at us.

12 A **cold / smelly / shiny** drink is perfect on a hot day.

Adjectives describe nouns.

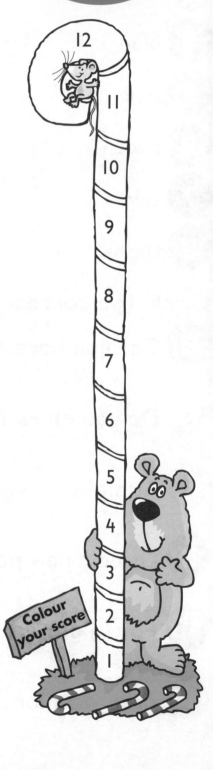

Colour your score

Adverbs

Underline the adverb in each sentence.

1 Ethan sang loudly.

2 James jogged slowly.

3 Nina ate quietly.

4 Jess spoke softly.

5 Kayla wrote quickly.

6 Zach swam smoothly.

7 Hannah drew carefully.

8 Oscar held on to the rope tightly.

Add **ly** to these words to make some adverbs.

9 bad + ly = _____

10 sudden + ly = _____

11 neat + ly = _____

12 cross + ly = _____

13 soft + ly = _____

14 kind + ly = _____

15 brave + ly = _____

Adverbs describe verbs. They often end in ly.

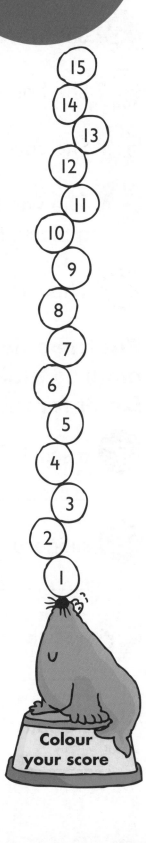

15
14
13
12
11
10
9
8
7
6
5
4
3
2
1

Colour your score

Noun phrases

Underline the noun phrase in each sentence.

1 The tall, pointed hat belonged to a witch.

2 She wore striped tights.

3 She had a long, sparkly wand.

4 She carried a secret spell book.

5 The witch had a friend who was a black, furry cat.

6 The cat had long, sharp claws.

Put the adjectives together with the noun to make a noun phrase. Don't forget commas!

7 a scarf   soft   warm

_____

8 slippery   icy   the path

_____

9 a stick   thin   long

_____

10 wobbly   a jelly   shaky

_____

A noun phrase can have adjectives as well as a noun.

Colour your score

28

Compound words

Write the two words that make up each compound word.

Breaking compound words down will help with your spelling.

1 grandmother

2 whiteboard

3 jigsaw

4 pancake

5 toothbrush

6 bathtub

7 rainbow

8 goldfish

Choose the correct word to make a new compound word.

| flower | bird | pan | fly | boy | ball |

9 sun _____

10 cow _____

11 butter _____

12 humming _____

13 sauce _____

14 snow _____

14
13
12
11
10
9
8
7
6
5
4
1 2 3

Colour your score

29

Suffixes: –ment and –ness

Make new words by adding the suffixes.

Root word	+ ment	Root word	+ ness
1 pave		**5** sad	
2 treat		**6** kind	
3 pay		**7** dark	
4 equip		**8** soft	

Choose a word to complete each sentence.

> **assortment movement appointment
> illness goodness rudeness**

9 My friend's _____ has put her in hospital.

10 I have an _____ at the doctor's.

11 The _____ of the boat made me feel sick.

12 "_____ me!" said the teacher.

13 They had a big _____ of sweets.

14 _____ makes my parents cross.

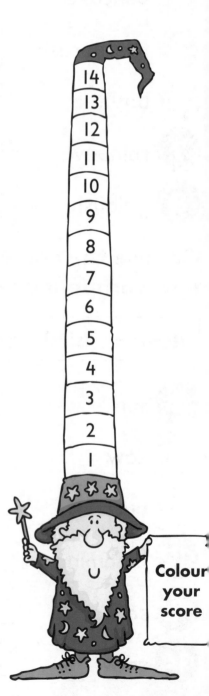

14
13
12
11
10
9
8
7
6
5
4
3
2
1

Colour your score

Word endings: –er and –est

Finish these word patterns.

1 rich, richer, _____

2 cold, _____, coldest

3 close, closer, _____

4 nice, _____, nicest

5 quick, quicker, _____

6 old, _____, oldest

7 high, higher, _____

8 warm, _____, warmest

Use these word endings for comparing things.

Choose a word to complete each sentence.

| smallest   sweeter   faster   largest |

9 I am small but Libby is the _____ girl in our class.

10 The lemon cake is sweet but the chocolate cake is _____.

11 A cheetah can run _____ than a dog.

12 The elephant is the _____ animal in the zoo.

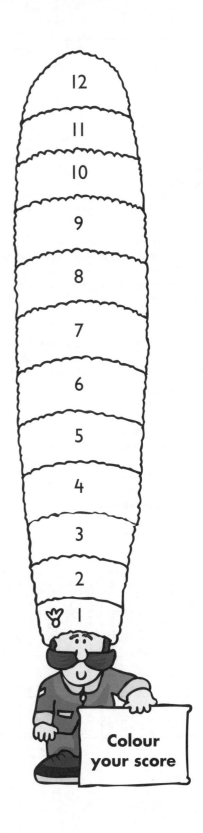

12
11
10
9
8
7
6
5
4
3
2
1

Colour your score

Answers

Context cues
1. sister
2. walk
3. picnic
4. flies
5. cricket
6. money
7. going
8. dishes
9. play
10. drums

Word building
1. sheep
2. coast / coats
3. might
4. shirt
5. sport
6. thing
7. chat
8. lunch
9. wind
10. snail / nails
11. tower
12. foil
13. boost / boots
14. shell
15. brick

Vowel digraphs
1. tail
2. cloud
3. blood
4. cheese
5. cloak
6. snail
7. tie
8. nail
9. coin
10. mouse
11. green
12. loop

Real or made-up?
Real words (in any order): shop, church, girl, frog, hill, door, week, walk
Made-up words (in any order): shup, grirk, zirn, frud, hild, druft, thurp

Rhyming words
1. band, hand
2. ring, king
3. cold, hold
4. wig, jig
5. let, pet
6. hook, book
7. sheep, keep

There are many acceptable answers for questions 8–15.
8. a word ending –en
9. a word ending –ip
10. a word ending –ut
11. a word ending –ill
12. a word ending –all
13. a word ending –oon
14. a word ending –unch
15. a word ending –ack

Common exception words

s	a	i	d	a	t	o	d	a	y
y	t	z	s	o	m	e	c	t	w
w	r	f	r	i	e	n	d	h	e
b	e	c	a	u	s	e	o	e	r
s	m	o	h	u	o	m	t	r	e
h	c	m	n	o	u	r	h	e	a
e	l	e	w	h	e	r	e	h	q
a	r	e	w	a	s	h	y	o	u

Sentences
1. I don't like washing my hair.
2. I clean my teeth every day.
3. At breakfast, I drink orange juice.
4. My sister can ride a bike.
5. We went to town on a bus. / We went on a bus to town.
6. He has lost his trainers.
7. Drink your milk.
8. They love baking cakes.
9. Can you help me?
10. I have broken my glasses.

Alphabetical order
1. a b c d
2. e f g i
3. h k l m
4. n o p q
5. r s t u w
6. v x y z
7. ball
8. radio
9. apple
10. gloves
11. fork
12. cup
13. bike
14. pencil
15. cushion

Word meanings
1. hat
2. carrot
3. pasta
4. shoes
5. pen
6. chair
7. ball
8. fridge
9. bed
10. fish

Features of stories
1. character
2. setting
3. plot
4. setting
5. plot
6. character
7. beginning
8. end
9. beginning
10. end

Comprehension
1. Goldilocks
2. Peeping in people's houses
3. In the woods
4. Yellow
5. Soft and red
6. She heard voices

Types of sentence
1. question
2. exclamation
3. command
4. statement
5. question
6. exclamation
7. command
8. Do you want to help me cook lunch?
9. What a mess you've made!
10. Put the book on the shelf.
11. I like cooking.
12. How many eggs do I need?

Present tense
1. watch
2. reads
3. use
4. loves
5. rains
6. sends
7. want
8. draws
9. fishing
10. singing
11. eating
12. cutting

Past tense
1. went
2. was
3. skipped
4. grew
5. dug
6. wrote
7. Yesterday, I went to school.
8. I ate spaghetti for lunch.
9. Last week, I saw a film at the cinema.
10. Last year, I flew to Canada.
11. My sister travelled to Liverpool.
12. I sang in a choir last month.

Correct sentences
1. ✓
2. ✗
3. ✓
4. ✗
5. ✗
6. ✓
7. ✗
8. ✗
9. ✗
10. ✓

Questions
1. Who
2. What
3. Where
4. Can
5. Which
6. How
7. Whose
8. Does
9. Will
10. Is

Exclamation marks
1. ✗
2. ✗
3. ✓
4. ✓
5. ✗
6. ✓
7. ✗
8. ✓
9. I eat cheese sandwiches.
10. I'm so angry with them!
11. My dad is the best dad in the world!
12. We will be there at 2 o'clock.
13. That's the best joke I have ever heard!
14. Don't do that!

Proper nouns
Capital letters needed (in any order):
Wales, Emily, Amsterdam, Wednesday, September, Dan, Arthur, India
Capital letters not needed (in any order):
apple, fork, car, sock, grass, feather, string

Commas in lists
1. We had to travel by car, boat, plane and train to get there.
2. He chose daisies, poppies, lilies and roses to plant in the garden.
3. Materials like metal, paper, glass and plastic can be recycled.
4. The drinks menu included coffee, water, juice and tea.
5. I bought new gloves, a scarf, a hat and a coat in the sale.
6. You will need paint, paintbrushes, a sketch book and glue.
7. France, Spain, Germany and Italy are countries in Europe.